Obviously FREE

TIPS TO LIVE WITH
Freedom and Grace

Lisa M. Padula

Obviously Free
Tips to Live with Freedom and Grace
©2016 Lisa M. Padula

Notice Of Rights
Manufactured in the United States of America. No part of this book may be reproduced, transmitted in any form or by any means—electronic, or mechanical—including photocopying and recording, or by any information storage or retrieval system, except as may be expressly permitted in writing by the publisher or author.

Notice Of Liability
The information in this book is distributed on an "as is" basis, for informational purposes only, without warranty. While every precaution has been taken in the production of this book, neither the copyright owner nor the publisher shall have any liability to any person or entity with respect to any liability, loss, or damage caused or alleged to be caused directly or indirectly by the information contained in this book.

Scripture quotations marked (TLB) are taken from the Holy Bible, New Living Translation, copyright ©1996, 2004, 2007, 2013 by Tyndale House Foundation. Used by permission of Tyndale House Publishers, Inc., Carol Stream, Illinois 60188. All rights reserved.

Scripture quotations marked (NASB) are taken from the New American Standard Bible®, Copyright © 1960, 1962, 1963, 1968, 1971, 1972, 1973, 1975, 1977, 1995 by The Lockman Foundation. Used by permission.

Scripture quotations marked (NIV) are taken from THE HOLY BIBLE, NEW INTERNATIONAL VERSION®, NIV® Copyright © 1973, 1978, 1984, 2011 by Biblica, Inc.® Used by permission. All rights reserved worldwide.

Scripture quotations marked (ESV) are from The Holy Bible, English Standard Version® (ESV®), copyright © 2001 by Crossway, a publishing ministry of Good News Publishers. Used by permission. All rights reserved.

Scripture quotations marked (KJV) are taken from the King James Bible, in the public domain.

ISBN-10: 1945464070
ISBN-13: 9781945464072

Published By:

Heritage Press Publications, LLC
PO Box 561
Collinsville, MS 39325

Contents

Foreword 1

Mirror, Mirror On the Wall 3

Put Down Your Backpack 5

Like Helium Balloons, Let Bitterness and Grudges Go 7

Stop Procrastinating 9

Keeping Your Promises 11

Blessed are the Peace Makers 13

Don't Worry, Be Thankful 15

A Few Minutes of Laughter 17

Keep Patience and Humility In Your Wardrobe 19

Just a Spoonful of Kindness Helps Everything Go Down 21

Practice Love 23

Get Convicted 25

This Little Light of Mine 27

No Camping Allowed 29

Notes 32

Living Obviously FREE 33

Obviously FREE ♡ Tips to Live with Freedom and Grace

Foreword

I have watched for many years all the "Let's be Thankful" challenges, "Grateful Challenges", "Attitude of Gratitude Day", "Love Day", "Kindness Week" etc. and so on posts in the media, on Facebook and just blatantly announced by folks. My mind has never quite understood this? Why have a title…Why post it? Why announce it? Why set only a week or day as our goal to love, be kind or be thankful? Should this so-called "thankfulness" be only during a season or during a challenge? Should it be like a New Year's resolution…that most people forget and give up on anyway?

I say a resounding, "NO!" As a believer in Christ I am convinced that we are encouraged, taught and basically commanded to be thankful. We need to pursue love and kindness. We should NOT need a challenge…We should NOT need a contest or even a certain attitude. And…it should not happen just "randomly"!

All we need to do is look around! Stand up…and realize what we already have…and not what we wish we had! Understanding that we are FREE from guilt and condemnation because of God's GRACE for us will change our lives. It is hard to remain mad, angry, bitter, depressed, ungrateful, unloving, annoyed or unkind when you believe this and live it.

So go ahead…say it…tell someone…tell God! Thank you!

Be purposeful and "obvious" in your thankfulness, forgiveness, patience, kindness and love toward others!

God's blessings are chasing you down…keep running the race toward your goal.

Obviously FREE ♡ Tips to Live with Freedom and Grace

I am choosing to live "obviously" FREE and purposefully walking…and I am praying that this little book will inspire you to live this way too!

Love,
Lisa

♡

Don't copy the behavior and customs of this world, but let God transform you into a new person by changing the way you think. Then you will learn to know God's will for you, which is good and pleasing and perfect.

Romans 12: 2 (NLT)

Obviously **FREE** ♡ Tips to Live with Freedom and Grace

Mirror, Mirror, On the Wall...

Understanding how much God loves us, how much He cares for us and how much GRACE He has extended to us by allowing Jesus to die on the cross for our sins…should make us better people. He has given us freedom! We are never so messed up that HE can't make us worthy. We have inherited His right standing. We are clean!

A new start…a new life!

He has extended to us forgiveness and love!

Do you understand this? Really "get" it? You will begin to genuinely view others through a different standard and react differently in your own daily life.

Obviously FREE ♡ Tips to Live with Freedom and Grace

OK…so what is stopping you?

SELF—Me, Myself and I

Most of us remember the question, "Mirror, mirror on the wall; who's the fairest of them all?" (from the story of Snow White)

C'mon…that is just a fairy tale. Who does this nowadays? Well we may not speak to mirrors but our egos and human nature still want to be self served. We still want to be the "fairest"…the best…number one!

False comparisons with others, prideful behavior, jealousy, I'm #1 attitudes, preoccupation with our performance, our looks, our money, our spouses, our children, our past actions…and the list goes on! Self examination is good. But only to the extent that it draws us closer to the realization that God loves us and sees us through the "lens" of Jesus Christ.

When we really see God's beautiful GRACE for us, we must consciously (purposefully) put off… "take off" so to speak, our old human nature habits and "put on" new ones.

Why? Because we can now stop looking in the mirror at ourselves and see that Jesus is the "fairest of them all!"

WOW…I can be FREE!

I will be thankful, accepting, forgiving, kind and loving today!

♡

You were taught with regard to your former way of life, to put off your old self, which is being corrupted by its deceitful desires; to be made new in the attitude of your minds; and to put on the new self, created to be like God in true righteousness and holiness.
Ephesians 4: 22-24

Obviously **FREE** ♡ Tips to Live with ℱreedom and 𝒢race

Put Down Your Backpack...

Imagine running a marathon with a 50lb. back-pack on your body? How well would you run? Could you finish the race? What if you crossed the finish line…only to discover that many others had dropped their packs along the way and enjoyed the run? These people looked around, saw the sights, heard the encouragement of the crowds, cheered other runners on and were basically exhilarated at their finish!

What??

When we insist on being solely in control of our own lives, destiny, feelings, decisions, situations and past problems…we become slaves. Slaves to carrying a heavy burden…a backpack loaded with weight that we were never meant to bear alone.

Obviously **FREE** ♡ Tips to Live with Freedom and Grace

Wow...you mean to tell me that I could have dropped this pack anywhere along the race? At the start? In the middle? Today?

Yup...

Living "obviously" FREE means grasping the truth that I have the power to put down, drop and lay aside these encumbrances of life. How do I know this? God tells me expressly so in His Word. And here's the great news...the more burdens that we let go of...the more God's GRACE covers us! What?

Yes...God's GRACE is only needed where we recognize sin and problems that need to be thrown off. YOU can be the blessed recipient of this wonderful gift!

Put down your Backpack...

♡

Therefore, since we are surrounded by such a great cloud of witnesses, let us throw off everything that hinders and the sin that so easily entangles, and let us run with perseverance the race marked out for us. Let us fix our eyes on Jesus, the author and perfecter of our faith...
Hebrews 12:1, 2a (NIV)

But where sin increased, grace increased all the more,
Romans 5: 20b (NIV)

Obviously **FREE** ♡ Tips to Live with *Freedom* and *Grace*

Like Helium Balloons, Let Bitterness and Grudges Go...

Like a helium balloon? What exactly does that mean?

Do you remember letting go of a balloon filled with helium as a kid? It went up, up and away! You could watch it for only so long and then it disappeared.

It is a choice to hold on to hurt. We store it away in our minds and nourish it by thinking about it, talking about it or rehashing it incessantly. There are also sometimes that we are not even aware that we are nursing a grudge because it is lodged so deeply in our hearts. But…grudges do affect us and everyone around us! They grow into bitterness and ruin our relationships. They may come to the surface and pop out at the worst possible moments. At their root they are selfish and damaging!

Go back to picturing that helium balloon…It was made to go up. Its purpose, when we let it go is to float away and out of sight! Letting go of resentment and grudges will allow you to grow into a better person. Forgiveness and resolving the issue (if possible), will allow you even greater freedom. This may sometimes be a long and hard process. Keep on keeping on! You will become more like God in this process. There will be more of HIM in your life and less of YOU. More of His peace…More of His joy…

Wow!

What a remarkable and wonderful opportunity to purposefully change your world! When I start to let go of things…it is only then that I really recognize God's GRACE towards me. I am living "obviously" FREE!

Bear with each other and forgive whatever grievances you may have against one another.
Colossians 3:13 NIV

𝒪𝒷𝓋𝒾ℴ𝓊𝓈𝓁𝓎 **FREE** ♡ Tips to Live with ℱreedom and 𝒢race

STOP
Procrastinating...

The only reason any of us would procrastinate or put off doing things is the belief that we have more time than we actually do. I can finish it tomorrow…I will do this or that later…I will finish the job then…I will tell them I love them next time that I see them…

Even the Bible warns us that our life is short. Like a mist or vapor to be exact! A vapor when measured is about 7 seconds long before it fades away. What a comparison! Procrastination limits our abilities, wastes our potential, robs us of our time, and weakens our relationships with others and God. It stresses us out and causes anxiety.

This is NOT the end of the story though. There is the good news!

When you begin to understand that you are so loved, given a brand new chance each day by God, and that His mercy is new for you each morning… You feel free to change. You are empowered to change! Procrastinators just lack discipline. Self discipline can be learned and practiced by every one of us. This is the really good news! Choose to make realistic daily schedules and goals and work diligently to finish them. Check them off as you go and thank God each time you complete a task. Limit your time for phone calls, tasks and shopping. Make decisions in a reasonable time period. Ask a good friend to keep you accountable and really listen to them.

You may have some failures at first…but do not procrastinate starting again!

What if tomorrow never comes?

Recognize that you are FREE from God's criticism, and covered by his unchanging and unswerving GRACE.

I don't know about you…but this truth always kicks me in the pants and spurs me on to use my time wisely and purposefully!

Why, you do not even know what will happen tomorrow. What is your life? You are a mist that appears for a little while and then vanishes.
James 4: 14 (NIV)

Obviously **FREE** ♡ Tips to Live with ℱreedom and 𝒢race

Keeping Your Promises...

We have all seen either on television or in real life a person taking an oath in a court of law. They place their right hand on the Bible and swear to tell the truth, the whole truth and nothing but the truth! If they break this promise they are breaking the law and can be prosecuted. Wouldn't it be amazing if we all really lived like this? If we broke our promises, or didn't tell the truth we could be held liable?

When we think of promises we often think of broken ones. How we have been disappointed, duped, fooled or hurt. There are after-affects, damaged hearts and consequences to not keeping our promises. Many children of dead-beat or absent parents can list from memory the file of broken promises that took place in their childhood.

Most broken marriages are a result of one or more unkept promises.

Obviously **FREE** ♡ Tips to Live with *Freedom* and *Grace*

NEWS FLASH

God never breaks His promises! He never has and He never will…

God looks at us with complete, unreserved GRACE and love, and challenges us to rest assured on His promises. His promises hold true even in the darkest of times. God never breaks His word. When God speaks…it's as good as it can get!

So…if we really believe this…if we choose to live with the recognition that we are "obviously" FREE in God's sight…shouldn't it change our behavior? When we truly understand what Christ did on the cross for us by keeping his promise of providing salvation, and He now looks at believers with such mercy and GRACE; it will be the motivation to follow his example.

We will choose to honor our promises to people…

We will keep our word no matter how tough it is to follow through…

We will realize that promises take effort, time and sacrifice…

We will realize that we are being purposefully thankful to God when we have the reputation of integrity and keeping our word with the people that we come in contact with.

The Lord is not slow in keeping his promise, as some understand slowness. He is patient with you, not wanting anyone to perish, but everyone to come to repentance.
2 Peter 3:9 (NIV)

Obviously **FREE** ♡ Tips to Live with ℱreedom and 𝒢race

Blessed are the Peace Makers...

Notice that I did not say "Blessed are the peace keepers?" Why?

Because peace keepers very often have the reputation as "yes men," door mats, or vacillating folks who just agree with everyone and never have an opinion of their own.

God calls us to be peace makers! We should behave in such a way as to make peace in most of life's situations (at least as far as it depends on us).

We CAN give our opinion…

Obviously **FREE** ♡ Tips to Live with *Freedom* and *Grace*

We CAN stand up when things are wrong or ungodly…

We CAN have an inner calm in the midst of life's trouble and trials…

We CAN also choose to "stand down" at times…

What? Stand down? Not give my opinion, thoughts or correct advice to people?

When I fully grasped God's total love and sacrifice for me by sending His son to die on the cross, it was then that I began to really get the concept of being a peace maker. It was not being a door mat, or wrung out dishrag, but trusting in God to give me the needed restraint in potentially "unpeaceful" times. It is possible!

Try asking the question "Who wants more peace in their life?" Everyone wants to have more peace! We all want an inner calm, stillness of life, and a tranquility of the soul. Who doesn't?

The Bible tells us to pursue it. In other words…pursue peaceful situations and solutions in your everyday schedules. Think before you speak or act! Choose your words wisely…Or choose NOT to use your words! Choose to comment if it will help…Or choose NOT to comment! Choose to mind your own business…or choose NOT to mind your own business! Choose to act if it will be beneficial…Or choose NOT to act!

I can choose to apply the same GRACE that God has shed on me, to others…

Blessed are the peacemakers, for they will be called sons of God.
Matthew 5: 9 (NIV)

Turn from evil and do good; seek peace and pursue it.
Psalm 34: 14 (NIV)

Obviously **FREE** ♡ Tips to Live with ℱreedom and 𝒢race

Don't Worry, Be Thankful...

We have more people, including children on anxiety medications than at any time in our history. Tranquilizers are not for emergency or extreme cases anymore… they have become the norm. Stress is at an all time high in our society and by our track record may only tend to get worse. I am not criticizing…just stating the facts. Yet the Bible still has some sound advice for our behavior when these troubling times do arise, and it is not just a mere oral prescription.

Part of the goal or message of this book is to encourage people to walk purposefully through life. Get it? That means on purpose…we give thanks. On purpose…we choose to compliment. On purpose…we look for the blessings. On purpose…we can realize that instead of carrying all the anxiety on our own, we can give it to God. On purpose…we realize that maybe we are growing and being stretched by the situations that are

Obviously FREE ♡ Tips to Live with Freedom and Grace

causing our worries. On purpose…we choose not to block out our feelings when we are anxious, but look for the lesson that we can only learn in times like these. On purpose…we practice NOT talking and thinking non-stop about our own personal situations. We recognize that this can become a selfish habit. WOW…

Tough thing to do, you must be thinking? An impossible way to conduct your life? Well…humanly speaking yes! But because of God's unmerited, free favor and gift of love for us we can have the power to do these things. You cannot buy it, borrow it or work hard for it…you just have to accept it by faith as a free gift. That's this thing called GRACE!

If we begin to view ourselves as "obviously" FREE from the powers and habits of this world and its worry-causing issues; we can purposefully survive anxious days. We can realize that God's GRACE has covered my bad days, as well as the good ones. This wonderful GRACE is actually multiplied on my anxious days because I may need it more. What a peaceful thought!

Do not be anxious about anything, but in everything, by prayer and petition, with thanksgiving, present your requests to God. And the peace of God, which transcends all understanding, will guard your hearts and your minds in Christ Jesus.
Philippians 4: 6, 7 (NIV)

Obviously **FREE** ♡ Tips to Live with Freedom and Grace

A Few Minutes of Laughter...

I know that laughter and joy are not the same concept. But try watching a group of little children being joyful and playful, and laughter will always be heard. It is great to have a joyful heart, but it is another thing to allow people to see it. A smiling face filled with laughter is a beautiful thing to behold. A minute of laughter can repair an hour full of sorrow.

Tune into social media, turn on the nightly news or read a daily newspaper and you will realize that life is very serious business. Natural disasters, fires, human tragedies, accidents and deaths seem to always be on the agenda. How can we enjoy life…let alone laugh?

Obviously FREE ♡ Tips to Live with Freedom and Grace

I can laugh because I am "obviously" FREE. I am free from having to suffer with all these scary things alone. God has promised to be with us through all of life's hard, tumultuous and trying circumstances. The question for you is…do you believe this?

If your answer is NO, then I can understand your fear and lack of joy or laughter. If your answer is YES and you still lack joy and laughter in your life, then something is wrong.

You may not really comprehend how much God loves you and is concerned with your life. He wants a personal relationship with all of us so that we can pray and call out to him with our sorrows, fears and anxieties. We can choose to leave them with Him…and still find joy in our times here on earth. We can live FREE from constant worry. Yes…we can choose to laugh. Really belly laugh and shake with exuberance! Laughter releases endorphins, increasing our sense of well-being. God created it!

So make your joy "obvious" and let it escape your heart and flow right out of your face!

Laugh…

♡

She is clothed with strength and dignity; she can laugh at the days to come.
Proverbs 31: 25 (NIV)

A cheerful heart is good medicine, but a crushed spirit dries up the bones.
Proverbs 17: 22 (NIV)

Obviously **FREE** ♡ Tips to Live with Freedom and Grace

Keep Patience and Humility in Your Wardrobe...

In a society that admires power, aggressiveness and a "me first" attitude, you can make a difference by keeping patience and humility at the front of your closet. By putting this picture in your mind, I want you to recall how you

Obviously **FREE** ♡ Tips to Live with *Freedom* and *Grace*

get dressed each day. We go to our closet and choose an outfit. We probably have many clothes to choose from, but we usually choose our best colors, best fitted and most flattering outfits. Who wouldn't?

When we truly understand the extent of God's beautiful gift of GRACE toward us, we will choose to put on patience and humility more often. Living "obviously" FREE means that we believe so strongly that God sees us through the lens of Jesus Christ…as beautiful and forgiven, that we start to view others in the same way. We are quick to extend GRACE to others. We have much more patience with people's short-comings because we know that God is patient with us. We keep our feet on the ground and our egos in check. We will not allow sinful pride and condescension to take over the way we behave toward people. We strive to put others first instead of ourselves!

When we take the outfits of patience and humility off the hangers each morning and clothe ourselves in them; we will enhance our relationships, enjoy better success in all areas, and have a healthy sense of peace and well-being. In essence, we start to look more like the person God desires us to be.

Do you want to wear the most flattering, best fitted and color coordinated outfit today? Keep patience and humility in the front of your closet…they go with everything!

♡

Be completely humble and gentle; be patient, bearing with one another in love.
Ephesians 4:2 (NIV)

Obviously **FREE** ♡ Tips to Live with ℱreedom and 𝒢race

Just a Spoonful of Kindness Helps Everything Go Down...

The amount of kindness that we put into people is equal to the measure of joy that we will receive back from them. It's not necessarily that people are trying to give joy back to us…but rather that we are choosing to view and treat them with kindness anyway. This can provide great happiness for us.

Obviously FREE ♡ Tips to Live with Freedom and Grace

It changes our viewpoint of people as well as their viewpoint of us. Like sugar helping medicine go down, kindness goes a long way towards making everything and everyone easier to handle.

God's kindness toward us while we are sinners is a wonderful example. His GRACE is a free gift that we cannot earn. His kindness and love is undeserved. He extends it with open arms anyway, in spite of who we are and how many rotten things we have in our history. This is GOOD news!

Can we live a kind existence in a mean world? Of course! The world may always be mean, and there will always be unkind people in it. Our actions should not be based on worldly views or opinions. Practice following these three steps…

1. Be "purposefully" kind in the face of meanness.

2. Be "purposefully" kind in spite of other people.

3. Be "purposefully" kind because God has shown kindness and love to us first.

Determine to write a note of encouragement, make a phone call, give a ride to work, visit an elderly or sick person, ask a lonely person for coffee or tea, compliment, smile at the cashier in the market, let someone cut in front of you at the store, hold the door, buy a coffee for the person behind you, give a gift for NO reason, bake a cake and deliver it, offer to babysit for a young couple, and here is the clincher…

Show kindness to someone who has been unkind to you!

♡

Make sure that nobody pays back wrong for wrong, but always try to be kind to each other and to everyone else.
1 Thessalonians 5: 15 (NIV)

Obviously **FREE** ♡ Tips to Live with ℱreedom and 𝒢race

Practice Love...

A coach in college once said to me, "Practice does not make perfect… it makes permanent!" Whatever we choose to practice daily or often will become a permanent fixture in the fabric of our lives. If your life was a coat of many colors…what would the fabric be adorned with? Hurts, sorrows, grudges, anger, bitterness, lies, gossip, deceitfulness, broken promises, unkept vows, depression, discouragement or fear?

"My coat does have all those things," you may be thinking. Well yes…of course. That is because you have been practicing them daily. But that is a fact that can change. It can change at any time in your life. It can change today!

Obviously FREE ♡ Tips to Live with Freedom and Grace

Jesus' death on the cross and subsequent resurrection was God's gift to you…and God's gift to me. By putting my faith and hope in this truth I can have complete forgiveness of my past. God's freely extended GRACE to mankind essentially washes our old coats (hearts) clean so that they can now be adorned differently. Our life's fabric can change with the beautiful hues of love. Not the mushy love, kisses, and flowers of romance…but a way to view people through God's eyes. This will change your world!

Remember this…

It is easy to love the loveable people. Cute, well-behaved children, pretty, smart, good smelling folks…yes, they're easy. Nice, kind and friendly neighbors, caring sales people, polite cashiers, cops who don't ticket us, and the very spiritual acting church goers. Yup…no problem! But this does not take any effort or reliance on God. This kind of love does not take any practice.

Try practicing love to the criticizing people who take joy in your mistakes. The grouchy neighbors, the badly behaved kid, the indigent person and that one annoying relative, are the ones that truly need the brand of love that only God can help us give. True love covers over people's faults and chooses to see the best in them. Unrequited love is our responsibility to a hurting world. It is our privilege to PRACTICE!!

This is love: not that we loved God, but that he loved us and sent his Son as an atoning sacrifice for our sins.

We love because he first loved us. If anyone says, "I love God," yet hates his brother, he is a liar. For anyone who does not love his brother, whom he has seen, cannot love God, whom he has not seen.
1 John 4: 10, 19, 20

Obviously **FREE** ♡ Tips to Live with Freedom and Grace

Get Convicted...

Have you ever been convicted? If you ask most people this question, they believe that you are asking them if they have ever been found guilty of a crime. That is one of the definitions of being convicted, but another meaning for conviction is a strong persuasion, feeling, compulsion or belief in something. Have YOU ever been convicted?

I personally have had many, many convictions! As a matter of fact, the reason I wrote this book is because I feel so strongly about God's amazing gift of GRACE and its significance for our lives, that I could not remain quiet. I felt moved…I felt compelled…I felt convicted!

Obviously FREE ♡ Tips to Live with Freedom and Grace

NEWS FLASH

Guilt and conviction are not defined as the same thing. Do not mix them up! Guilt moves you for a while to do or change something, especially when people are observing you…and conviction produces and spurs you on to true change and permanent action (even when no one is watching).

When you trust in Jesus Christ and develop a personal relationship with God…the Holy Spirit becomes your inner guide. It is that small, quiet voice that moves us to act and behave in certain ways. The more that we really recognize that God loves us and wants the best for us the more we will stay in tune to HIS inner leading. Our convictions will come from God and motivate us to purposefully act and live. Looking to God's Word for guidance will be the base of our convictions. If I need to seek forgiveness from someone…I will do it. If I need to drop my bitter attitude…I will strive to look to God for help. If I am selfishly jealous of someone else…I will learn to be more thankful for what I do have. If I seem to have a low self esteem…I will strive to grasp the fact of God's freeing, wonderful GRACE and how HE views me. Wow…our lives can be so much more fulfilling and FREE when our convictions come from God!

So we keep on praying for you, asking our God to enable you to live a life worthy of his call. May he give you the power to accomplish all the good things your faith prompts you to do. Then the name of our Lord Jesus will be honored because of the way you live, and you will be honored along with him. This is all made possible because of the grace of our God and Lord, Jesus Christ.
11 Thessalonians 1: 10-12

Obviously **FREE** ♡ Tips to Live with Freedom and Grace

This Little Light of Mine...

How is your light burning? Is there anything worth getting passionate about?

This lack of passion plagues many folks nowadays and probably always has plagued us down through time. True faith in God and His plan for us requires real passion. Real purpose and dedication! Get passionate…

A life lived on purpose is not a fad to be taken up for one year and then dropped the next. It lasts. It has been tested over the generations and centuries and societies of history. It works! But passion does not happen accidentally. We do not just float into becoming passionate about anything. It is a determined pursuit!

If you study the ancient Olympic Games in Greece, there was a relay race where a lighted torch was passed. The goal was to reach the finish line as fast as possible without the fire going out. The ritual aspect of running with the lighted torch without extinguishing it was far more important than the competition itself. It was an honor to be chosen to carry the torch and the runners took the responsibility to keep it lit very seriously. The Greek torch race inspired the introduction of the Olympic flame at the Berlin games of 1936.

Hmm…I want to finish well. Do you? I do not want to just limp across the line half-heartedly with my torch extinguished. Even if you or I stumble and fall, we can look to God for help, and allow His spirit to keep our light and passion burning. We get back up, dust ourselves off and trust Him with our circumstances.

That's what I want! That is how I am going to purposefully and "obviously" live!

Will you also choose to live with a flame of passion in your soul for the world to see?

Let us strive to finish the race with our torches burning!

♡

When Jesus spoke again to the people, he said, "I am the light of the world. Whoever follows me will never walk in darkness, but will have the light of life."
John 8: 12

In the same way, let your light shine before men, that they may see your good deeds and praise your Father in heaven.
Matthew 5: 16

Obviously **FREE** ♡ Tips to Live with Freedom and Grace

No Camping Allowed...

When I was a young girl my family used to go camping for our vacations. We camped in Colorado, Wyoming, Montana, Kentucky and all over the country. In very many of the campgrounds, especially in the dangerous

Obviously **FREE** ♡ Tips to Live with *Freedom* and *Grace*

places in the west you would see "No Camping Allowed" signs. Sometimes these seemed like the coolest and most picturesque spots to set your tent on. Why would they say "No Camping"? Usually if you took the time to read the small print on the bottom of the sign there would be many valid reasons to obey. Rock slides, dangerous cliffs, flooding rivers, wild animals and bears could be listed among the dangers. If you did NOT follow the sign your personal safety might be at stake.

Hmm…as I pondered these memories I realized that I myself had camped and erected my tent in many places that God had clearly posted a "No Camping Allowed" warning. No, I didn't actually set up a tent and there was no real sign posted anywhere…but I have paused and stopped long enough in some troubling areas in my life that it seemed like I had camped there. Maybe you have too!

Think about it…God's Word, the Bible is full of advice about places that we should NOT choose to reside at. What? Where?

How about anger, envy, bitterness, hate? (Ephesians 4:31)

What about fear and troubles in the future? (John 16:33)

How about worry? (Matthew 6:25, Philippians 4:6)

There are signs about grumbling and complaining? (Philippians 2:14)

Being a busy-body? Not being a gossiper? (1 Thessalonians 4:11)

Maybe you are camped in the "lack of discipline" area? (1Timothy 4:7)

Could you be camped in guilt? Trapped there by your past?

There are signs all throughout the Bible on places that we should NOT set up our tent and choose to live. Staying in these places can only cause trouble and danger to our very lives and souls. It may be time to take a better look at your camp-site and discern if you need to pull up the stakes and move on.

Obviously FREE ♡ Tips to Live with ℱreedom and 𝒢race

Will this be easy? Nope…not one bit! But you will not have to go it alone. God can and will be with you every step of the way if you ask Him, call to Him, and let Him move you. His wonderful and freeing GRACE will enable you with the strength to pull up stakes and move out. God will NOT force you to move though. You have a free will and it is often very stubborn. Your only job is to just "let go" of the ground that you might be holding on so tightly to…pull up those stakes…stomp out the campfire and let God move your tent! Signs, signs…everywhere are signs.

Is God is telling you "No Camping Allowed" where you are? If so…it's time to pack up the tent and move on! Better sites are up ahead and you are FREE to camp there!

♡

For YOU have been a refuge for me, a tower of strength against the enemy. Let me dwell in YOUR tent forever; let me take refuge in the shelter of your wings.
Psalm 61:3, 4 (NASB)

Obviously FREE ♡ Tips to Live with Freedom and Grace

Notes

I need to work on:

Obviously FREE ♡ Tips to Live with Freedom and Grace

Living Obviously FREE...

Obviously FREE ♡ Tips to Live with Freedom and Grace

So…this whole book boils down to this one premise…this one question. "Do you understand and accept that God's wonderful GRACE and mercy makes you FREE in His sight?" He sent His son to die on the cross to give us salvation from our sins and salvation from the daily grind and pressures of life here on earth. Our only act is to just accept it! By faith you can choose to believe this truth and it will radically transform your life.

"Oh…but what about all the other crap in my life" you may be thinking? Here is the good news. No…here is the great news! Your past doesn't shock him…and your present will never worry Him. We are never too messy, too broken, or too sinful that HE can't make us worthy and full of value! He washes us in His mercy…we are clean in His sight. And by the way…our future may be a mystery or scary to us, but it is never a mystery to God! He is already there! He is the beginning and the end of life!

WOW…!

Living "obviously" FREE is demonstrated when you believe this fact and run your race in life with perseverance. Run and live each day with determination and purpose! We do not just randomly be kind, thankful, forgiving and loving; we do it on purpose…with a purpose! This does not mean we have perfected our life, it just means that we keep going. We do not quit when we see the long journey before us. We are not just resigned to trudge onward or fall into a boring pattern year after year. NO! Freedom in God's sight should push us, motivate us to live triumphantly and alive.

Our race can be freely run because this race becomes God's plan for our lives, not ours!

Once again I will state the original question…"Why desire to live your life FREE and purposefully?"

For me personally, I want to persevere with a strong faith and purpose daily, because I want to finish well! I want to cross that finish line with my torch held high in the air and still burning brightly!

Obviously FREE ♡ Tips to Live with Freedom and Grace

If this could be my last day…I want it to be my best day!

I will strive to live "obviously" FREE and walking with a purpose for the sake of all who I encounter and influence. If you and I keep our hearts set in this direction, we can indeed become people who live passionately for God!

So go ahead, throw your arms up like you are in the front seat of a roller coaster because you now have…GRACE and FREEDOM as your fellow riders in life!

♡

I have fought the good fight, I have finished the race, I have kept the faith.
2 Timothy 4:7

Now the Lord is the Spirit, and where the Spirit of the Lord is, there is freedom.
2 Corinthians 3:17

Notes

I am thankful for:

www.ingramcontent.com/pod-product-compliance
Lightning Source LLC
Chambersburg PA
CBHW071549080526
44588CB00011B/1838